ACKNOWLEDGEMENTS:

There are so many people to tited
space for acknowledgements, for
opening doors for me and tho
bringing this book to life.

Robert Kiyosaki, the author of **"Rich Dad, Poor Dad."**
I've learnt so much about business and investing through your
books, and your influence has inspired me to write this book.

I obviously thank my parents for understanding my
vision even though it sounded crazy to them at the beginning.
Thanks for your love and support.

Zorro, you know I can't forget how you want out of your
way to print rough drafts of this book when I didn't have a
printer of my own. Angie, remember when you used to say I'll
make it one day? I guess that day has come huh. Tannie and
Tadiwa, life's tough so wear a helmet. Praise thanks for the
support, words can't explain how much I appreciate it. My
brothers and sisters, Neville, Charles, Michael, Bellamy,
Takunda, Kevin, Coleen, Patience, Petty, and Steven, I love you
guys. My little brothers Lavern and William, this book is for
you. My cousins Kuda Mujikwa, Kuda (manager), Tatenda,
Ernest, Tapiwa, Tsitsi, Jonas, Lawna, I hope you enjoy this
book.

My friends Carolina, Natalie, Maureen, Nadia, Kyla,
Vicky, Kristina, Lisa, Sherri, Careena, Rachael, Anilla, Tari,
Nayoka, Simmone, Leigh and Tamara, thanks for supporting
me ladies. I can't forget Tranessa, Farai, Simba, Junior, Chris,

1

Troy, Andrew, Nicky, Russell, Primrose and Joe. Hey Tunga, I had to do it to them with this book.

Lennox and Lester, I really admire you guys. Weird, Bang Out and Loxamillion, I can't wait to see you guys blowing up. Pee Kay thanks for showing me love man. The world isn't ready for the heat you'll be bringing on your album. Noel I love what you've done for the Rich Rapper website. Let's do it again on future projects.

If I missed anyone...remind me to add you in the next book.

Rich Rapper, Poor Rapper

Why Less Talented Artists Get Ahead-
And Everyone Else Is Left Looking For A
Record Deal

Hilary Mujikwa

4

Table of Contents

LESSONS

BEGINNINGS

Rich Rapper, Poor Rapper

CHAPTER 1

Rich Rapper, Poor Rapper

As narrated by Hilary Mujikwa

I Personally know two great rappers in Florida. I refer to them as rich rapper and poor rapper. They are both very passionate about their music. One of them is both a rapper and a producer that has made beats for many independent rappers.

The other doesn't know how to make beats and often needs assistance from different beat makers to complement his song writing style.

One of the rappers is very articulate. He speaks in a clear tone using big words that many of us don't know exist in the English language. He was also an "A" student in high school.

The other rapper was born in an African country called Zimbabwe. Now as you and I both know. Zimbabwe is not known as the home of the biggest rap artists in the world. If anything, the image most people have in their minds about Africa is clay huts, topless women with pieces of cloth covering their genital areas and naked men with spears chasing zebras. I know my last statement sounds silly but that's the kind of thinking he had to confront.

He was also a straight "C" student at best in high school that made the "B" grade once in a blue moon. Furthermore, his lack of concentration in class caused him to fail most of his exams because when everybody was taking notes in class, he found himself writing songs that he wanted the world to sing.

Both of these rappers are great people with high expectations in life. They both want the world to hear their music and are looking for ways to expose their music to the world. The difference between them is their financial situation and the way they think.

The artist I call poor rapper finds himself borrowing clothes and jewelry from friends when he needs to look extra nice at big events. He not only struggles with his wardrobe, but at the end of the month when the bills are due, he barely has enough money to keep the lights on. There have been instances when the electricity in his house was cut off.

When that happened he would simply turn the power back on illegally. He would do this by stealing a mechanical device used by electricity companies to power private homes, and connect the device to the power generator in his house.

The other artist that I refer to as rich rapper enjoys a completely different lifestyle. Even though both rich rapper and poor rapper don't have major record deals, rich rapper is constantly receiving free clothes from designer clothing lines. He never has to borrow clothes because some of the companies that manufacture clothes want their clothing to be seen on rich rapper.

I won't lie to you and tell you that he doesn't have financial problems too, because he does. He just has different types of money problems which include paying his advisers for advice, buying large quantities of CDs and paying expensive shipping costs to many parts of the world. These things require capital but rich rapper is willing to do whatever it takes to make it happen.

Observing the contrasting ways rich rapper and poor rapper thinks, has helped me get a better understanding of why rich rapper is more successful than poor rapper. For example, one of the rappers makes good music and sends it to A&R people hoping to get a record deal. The other rapper thinks that's a complete waste of time and postage stamps.

One of the rappers travels around the country rubbing shoulders with record industry people, trying to slide them a copy of his demo. The other rapper meets record executives and never bothers to hand his music out to them because he doesn't care too much for a record deal.

Another noticeable difference between the two rappers is the subject of fame. One rapper wants his face to be all over billboards and magazines so that everybody knows who he is. He wants to be a ghetto superstar who demands attention wherever he goes. Yet the other rapper doesn't really want to be in the spot light. He just wants the world to hear his music so they can buy his CD and listen to it in the comfort of their own homes.

Now as you can tell, both rappers love their music but their approach to the music business is completely different. I guess that's why the less talented rapper from Zimbabwe is more successful than the articulate rapper who is a talented producer.

Rich rapper might have been one of the worst students in high school, who helped make the top of the class happen. But his willingness to change his thoughts and habits from those of poor rapper has made all the difference in his life.

Awaking The Genius In Rich Rapper

CHAPTER 2

Awaking The Genius In Rich Rapper

Before rich rapper started finding success in the music business, he and poor rapper would spend a lot of time together. During week days, when everybody else was working. They would both be drinking and smoking in a pre-production studio while discussing what they were going to do when someone gave them a major record deal.

If they were not getting high they would be watching music video's, complaining about why less talented artists seemed to get all the lucky breaks, while real hip hop artists like themselves didn't. The real hip hop with the best crafted lyrics which they specialized in wasn't generating any money for them. There's nothing pretty about 2 grown men in their 20's living in their parents' homes and being stone broke all the time. Life really sucks when you're broke.

To cover up their frustration they would often complain about "garbage rappers getting record deals." Life just didn't seem fair to them. They would say things like "These commercial rappers are killing hip hop" and "That music getting so much air play isn't real hip hop, we should make that real hip hop and send it to A&R people that will give us a record deal".

Now as you can tell both rich rapper and poor rapper were frustrated with the results they were getting. Everyday, poor rapper would work on new beats and would send them off to record companies, along with a few songs he had recorded in hopes of getting signed. Unfortunately, none of the record companies ever called him. I think it would be safe to say they were not interested.

To be fair to poor rapper, I won't neglect to mention that rich rapper was also struggling. He couldn't make beats to save his own life. Whenever rich rapper needed beats to write to, he would have to pay poor rapper to create the beats for him. He still can't make beats to this day but he's an excellent lyricist who can make a song about any subject matter. Just don't ask him to make you a beat because asking him to do so is like asking a pig to sing and I've yet to see that happen.

The life changing experience that awoke the genius in rich rappers heart was when he took his first trip to New York. He, poor rapper and friends had been working together trying to figure out how they could get a record deal with the help of two entrepreneurs.

These entrepreneurs had built a movie production company along with a few other public companies which they financed. They drove fancy cars that most people only dream about owning and had flashy mansions and pent houses that are worth millions. Rich rapper felt blessed to be afforded the opportunity to stay in their house while he was in New York.

The next morning after he arrived in New York, he woke up to the sweet sound of birds singing. It was eleven o'clock on a week day after most people had already rushed off to work. Rich rapper was surprised to find the entrepreneurs at home wearing expensive night gowns, sitting at the breakfast table, enjoying their morning watching a program on CNN.

This surprised rich rapper because in his mind he was thinking "I can't believe this! Why are these two gentlemen still at home at 11 in the morning looking like they just woke up? Most people get up early to get to work by 9 am and hope to put in a little overtime." This thought puzzled him as he had breakfast with the entrepreneurs.

After breakfast the entrepreneurs invited rich rapper into their home office. It was a big room with two classy office desks which where surrounded by framed posters of huge hit movies on the walls. These were movies they had worked on. Rich rapper was amazed at how calm the entrepreneurs were when they started discussing the millions they were making through their movies alone.

This blew rich rappers mind because these multi millionaire's where still in their morning gowns, relaxing at home and making more money than he would if he went around the world doing live shows in every city that would pay him to perform.

Now I'm not saying that money is the most important thing in the world but it has a way of making life a lot easier. So for that very same reason, I can understand why rich rapper was motivated to get out of the sad financial situation he and poor rapper were in.

Rich rapper then sat in an empty chair, in the home office and observed the entrepreneurs in action. They were making calls to bankers, lawyers, accountants, business people, and famous artists who hang out with the successful actors they were in business with.

Rich rapper didn't know what to make of all this but he was certain that these guys were not making money the traditional way. They seemed to be in control of their lives and the way they spoke demanded respect.

Rich rapper didn't know exactly what these guys were talking about on the phone but he knew he wanted to do what they were doing. He was tired of being a talented rapper with nothing to show for it. And even though the entrepreneurs were in the film industry, he made a decision to learn all he could from them.

Stars Are Created, Not Born

CHAPTER 3
Lesson One:

Stars Are Created, Not Born

It dawned on rich rapper, that the entrepreneurs were on the phone with some of Hollywood's elite group of people. This was a dream come true for him. It's not everyday that an unsigned artist can have access to some of Hollywood's 'A' list actors.

When the entrepreneurs got off the phone they asked rich rapper how they could best assist him in the music business. This seemed like the moment rich rapper had been waiting on for so many years. He was finally going to get the record deal that he dreamed about. Rich rapper replied "Well, you have listened to my demo and you think it's good. I'm glad you like my music but I would love for the world to hear my music. I want a record deal."

Rich rapper then began explaining how he felt about the music on the air waves. He even told them that he thought his music was better than most of the "garbage" that was out at the time.

The entrepreneurs seemed to be paying close attention to every word that came out of rich rappers mouth. It was as if they were studying his body language. Then one of them softly said "We love your music. I even let my wife hear it and she loved it too. There is no doubt in my mind that you're a very talented rapper."

A wide smile came across rich rappers face as he said to him self "I'm going to be a mega star. I can see it happening already."

I can only imagine how excited rich rapper must have been to be finally getting one of his biggest dreams come true. This was the day that he had been dreaming about for years!

The entrepreneurs then stated "You're a great rapper but you are not a star yet. Stars are created…not born." Rich rapper was stunned by that statement.

He almost fell out of his seat as he asked "What do you mean by stars are created and not born? Don't you know that we, artists come up with original ideas to put good music together? We were born to be stars and we deserve fair compensation for our hard work."

The entrepreneurs quietly sat there as if looking for the right words to say. Then one of them politely replied

"An artist only becomes a star when willing customers are paying for their music. I realize that you're a talented rapper who the world needs to hear but unfortunately the business doesn't work that way. The people with the money make the rules."

Rich rapper didn't like what he heard but he realized that there was a lesson to be learnt here. He responded "Isn't that unfair to the artists? I mean we work so hard to come up with innovative music and look how we're treated."

"I can understand why you think artists are treated unfairly" replied the entrepreneurs. "But do you realize that in order for a talented rapper to become a house hold name in hip hop requires capital? Somebody has to pay for the marketing, promotion and distribution of your music and that money doesn't just fall out the sky."

Rich rapper had never thought about that before. He thought that an artist just had to record a demo in the studio and if his music was good enough he would get a record deal and become rich, just like the way it appears in the movies.

"If life was so simple we wouldn't have so many ruined artists who have never been signed" continued the business owners. "This might be one of the reasons why many artists hate the music industry so much."

Rich rapper then slowly learned forward in his chair and said "Ok, so what you're telling me is that no matter how talented I am as a rapper, the record company that signs me is going to be calling the shots?" "Well it depends on how you position yourself" replied the business owners.

"Not everybody is told what to do in the business world. There are different rules for different types of people. Some artists find themselves being forced to make records they don't like and barely make ends meet because their label is telling them what to do. While other artists have the freedom to do as they please with their music plus have the privilege of enjoying the luxuries money has to offer."

Before rich rapper could respond, one of the entrepreneurs grabbed the phone on his desk, dialed a number and turned the speaker phone on.

Rich rapper couldn't believe his ears. One of the key decision makers from Motown records was on the phone. This seemed almost too good to be true. The entrepreneurs were telling the label head about him, as the excitement of this once in a lifetime opportunity flowed through his veins. Could this be the big break he had been waiting for?

After having a brief conversation, the entrepreneurs told the label head that rich rapper was looking for an internship at their company. The label head saw no problem with rich rapper joining their fabulous team, so he referred rich rapper to his business affairs manager, who was to see rich rapper that very same day.

Rich rapper wasn't thrilled about being an intern at Motown. He wanted a record deal, not a corporate job! So as soon as the label head got off the phone rich rapper asked, "Why did you tell him I want to be an intern? I really need a record deal."

The entrepreneurs looked rich rapper in the eye and replied, "When you are needy you're weak. Don't be so weak man. Needy people usually finish last in the game of life. Don't you know that there is an abundance of opportunity out there?"

Rich rapper didn't understand what they meant by being weak when you're needy. All he knew was that he needed that record deal because as far as he was concerned, there was no other way for his music to be heard.

"How can being an intern help me become a better rapper?" he asked himself.

As if the entrepreneurs could read his mind, they quickly said "When you're needy you're weak. If you don't believe us, just watch reality TV shows like 'American Idol' and 'Making of the Band.' Notice how desperate the artists on those shows are to get signed. When you're living in a world of lack you tend to settle for anything life tosses your way. You could be getting a pathetic deal that makes no sense financially and if all you see is a world of scarcity, you'll probably jump onto the first deal you're offered"

"What the heck are these guys trying to say about artists auditioning for reality TV shows?" thought rich rapper. He detested the entrepreneurs calling him weak.

He instantly yelled "Not everybody is rich like you guys, you know. If unsigned rappers don't get a record deal then how are we supposed to make the big bucks that you guys are making?"

"That's a great question" responded the entrepreneurs. "You're starting to ask questions which require a lot of thinking. Many rappers run through life without thinking where their careers are headed."

"They run through life without thinking. Are you saying many artists are stupid?"

The entrepreneurs laughed as they replied "No that's not what we're saying. The idea of recording a demo and sending it to record labels or music producers like Puffy and Missy Elliot is a good idea for most rappers.

But that isn't the only way to make it into the business you're trying to get into."

"What are you guys trying to tell me" mumbled rich rapper. "I have seen successful artists on television shows like 'American Idol' and 'Making the Band' getting record deals. All they had to do was convince the judges to sign them."

Rich rapper was puzzled by the entrepreneurs point of view so he asked "Why don't you think too highly of those television shows?"

The entrepreneurs smiled because rich rappers facial expression revealed that he sincerely wanted to know what was on their minds.

"Making the Band' and 'American Idol' are great television programs. They do a great job of keeping the public entertained. However, the image they portray of artists isn't necessary true. Not every artist is told what to do and what kind of music to make by record producers. The myths these shows have brought to the table are robbing many artists from becoming successful."

Before Rich rapper could ask any more questions, one of the entrepreneurs phone rang. They had to get on a conference call, so therefore the discussion they were having with rich rapper had to wait until later.

Rich rapper had so many more questions to ask. His mind had begun to open up to a new world he never knew existed before then.

He was now determined to find out what made the entrepreneurs so knowledgeable about business and music. What was it about these entrepreneurs that made them far more successful than the average person? Why were these guys making so much money without having to work overtime like everyone else?

Yacht Money or Canoe Money

CHAPTER 4

Lesson Two:

Yacht Money or Canoe Money

When the entrepreneurs were done with their conference call, they asked rich rapper to get ready for his Motown appointment.

"When you arrive you're going to see the business affairs manager. The label head won't be there, so make sure you're on your best behavior," explained the entrepreneurs.

Rich rapper didn't have a problem with that because as far as he was concerned this was his perfect opportunity to let Motown hear his music.

While in the car with the entrepreneurs, who were giving rich rapper a ride to the train station, the entrepreneurs asked "Do you want yacht money or canoe money?"

Rich rapper understood that purchasing a yacht required more money than buying a canoe. Who in their right state of mind would settle for a canoe if they can afford a yacht? "I want yacht money" he replied in a confident tone.

"It's great to know that you're ambitious. Many rappers choose to earn canoe money. If you're really serious about making yacht money, you need to stop looking for a record deal."

"Stop looking for a record deal?" screamed rich rapper in amazement.

"Yea, stop needing one so badly. Listen closely to what we're telling you because this is what makes the difference between rappers like Puffy and artists that aren't too successful. The richest rappers in the world control their own destiny in the music business. No one tells them what kind of music to make and they don't go around looking for a record deal. They choose to create deals that make sense to them instead. That's why you see P Diddy and Jay Z calling their own shots. They aren't on their hands and knees begging for a record deal are they?"

Rich rapper didn't completely understand what he was being told. But he often wondered why rappers like P Diddy, Jay Z and Master P were making hundreds of millions of dollars, while many rappers were complaining about their record label.

In his opinion, his favorite rappers were better than P Diddy and Master P. But why were rappers like Diddy and Master P more successful than the artists he preferred? It was strange to him.

As they were getting closer to the train station, one of the entrepreneurs slowly stated "The decision to make yacht money or canoe money is ultimately yours. Your vote is the only one that counts. Consciously or unconsciously every rapper chooses their own path. Today, we're giving you the opportunity to see the other side of the coin. Are you wiling to learn everything you need to know to make yacht money?"

Rich rapper nodded his head and instantly said "I want to learn everything there is to know about yacht money. Tell me about the other side of the coin."

"Ok" replied the entrepreneurs. "If you're really serious about making yacht money, don't pass your demo out to anyone at Motown. When you arrive, tell the business affairs manager you want to be an intern because you want to learn the business. Is that understood?" Rich rapper nodded his head in agreement, even though the thought of not handing out his demo hurt his feelings.

The entrepreneurs then said "ok, I guess we have an understanding. We don't want you to tell anybody at the label that you plan on releasing your own records because you need to learn everything you can about the business. That's how P Diddy got into the business and we believe you have the potential to make the same moves he's making."

The entrepreneurs continued explaining the importance of learning different aspects of the music business. It was a great eye opening experience that changed the way rich rapper thought about the subject of business forever.

Life's Tough So Wear a Helmet

CHAPTER 5

Lesson Three:

Life's Tough So Wear a Helmet

The train ride to Manhattan was long and boring, but Rich rapper was too excited to worry about that. He was happy to be getting the chance of a lifetime. It's not everyday that someone at a record label like Motown is waiting to see you.

When he finally arrived, he was truly impressed. The inside of the label was surrounded by TV's playing nothing but Motown music videos. Rich rapper had seen plenty of Motown videos but he hadn't realized how large their catalog was. He couldn't help but wonder how Motown could afford to develop and market so many artists. "This is amazing" he whispered to himself.

At that exact moment the secretary who was at the front desk snapped rich rappers train of thought and asked "How can I help you." Rich rapper explained to her that he had come to see the business affairs manager.

"Sure, please wait here while I get her" insisted the secretary.

After about five minutes of waiting, a beautiful light skinned woman with pretty brown eyes and a gorgeous smile introduced herself to rich rapper. It was the business affairs manager. She was wearing casual clothes that looked really good on her.

I think rich rapper found this lady very attractive and was wondering how a young lady like her could possibly be the business affairs manager of such a big record company.

The young lady then assisted rich rapper to her office and asked him to take a seat. Rich rapper was glad to finally take a seat because he had been doing a lot of walking from the train station to the label. That's hard work if you don't exercise much.

The business affairs manager then smiled and asked "I heard you're from the continent of Africa, what part are you from?" "I'm from a country in the southern part of Africa called Zimbabwe" replied rich rapper.

"I've heard so much about Africa. I would love to go there someday" said the business manager with a wide smile on her face. She then started telling a story about one of her bosses being from another African country that is located in the western part of Africa. She spoke very highly about her boss, just like any loyal employee seeking a promotion would. I guess that's why Rich rapper silently sat in his chair and listened to her senseless ass kissing technique.

The business manager then started talking about herself and all the hard work she had done at the label. She told rich rapper about how she constantly receives calls from people who want to use images of Motown artists to promote their own businesses.

She then got carried away and started telling rich rapper how excited she was about Brian McKnight joining their label. Rich rapper couldn't do anything except listen to this fine woman expressing her excitement about her job.

After she was done talking she asked rich rapper about his work experience. Rich rapper didn't have much work experience. The only two jobs he held were telemarketing and driving a van for a pharmacy that needed to have medication delivered to their customers. Now as you've already guessed, the business affairs manager wasn't too impressed with rich rappers work experience. She then asked "What collage did you graduate from?" "I attended collage but unfortunately couldn't graduate because of personal reasons" replied rich rapper.

He couldn't help but feel a little uneasy because of the way she was watching his every move. Her response was "We don't normally hire people without collage degrees and you don't have much work experience either."

Those truthful words sent a chill down his spine and poked the depths of his personal soul. "Why does it have to be this way?"

Rich rapper didn't like what was going on. "Is this lady saying I can't intern because I don't have a collage degree?" he asked himself. "Is she trying to say because I don't have a piece of paper, I'm a piece of shit whose life will amount to nothing?" This really bothered rich rapper.

The business affairs manager continued talking about all the great things she had done at the label once again. She started telling rich rapper how she started as an intern and climbed the corporate ladder until she got the position she was in. She continued putting even more emphasis on her job title and collage degree which she proudly said gave her a solid foundation for the future.

I don't blame her for feeling the way she did because she strongly believed in having a safe and secure job with benefits. Her goal was to climb the corporate ladder all the way to the top, while collage drop outs like rich rapper struggled to get an internship.

Rich rapper was beginning to get annoyed. In his opinion, "The business affairs manager was looking down on him." What was he supposed to do, go back to collage for many more years? I hate to be the one to tell you, but that would be very out of character for Rich Rapper. The only thing he liked about school was picking up collage girls.

The business manager then thanked rich rapper for coming to see her. She proceeded to tell rich rapper how she really enjoyed talking to him and would be giving him a call soon. Now it doesn't take a genius to figure out that she wasn't going to call. But rich rapper played along with her little game.

He knew the business affairs manager didn't see him as corporate material. He had no choice but to swallow the bitter pill life had shoved down his throat.

Why Climb The Corporate Ladder If You Can Build One?

CHAPTER 6

Why Climb The Corporate Ladder If You Can Build One?

When Rich rapper got back to the entrepreneurs house, he found them busy at work. He didn't want to bother them so he decided to spend most of his time in the guest room.

The thought of the business affairs manager making him feel so inferior was still tormenting him. "How could a person about my age be so much more successful than I am?" he asked himself. "What am I doing wrong?"

He began to think about all the things his mother said about pursing a career in music. She wasn't really thrilled about him pursuing music. Most of the artists she knew were not doing too well financially, so being the concerned mother she was, she wanted the best for her son. In her opinion, "She would have been more excited about her son pursuing law or something along those lines." Rich rapper couldn't help but wonder if he had made the right life choices?

The next day when rich rapper had finished packing to head back to Florida, he told the entrepreneurs how he felt. He explained how far behind he felt because he didn't have a collage degree, and to make matters worse he still he wasn't making any money with his music. He had never felt this discouraged before.

The entrepreneurs then said "We can understand how you feel right now. There have been times when we've felt discouraged ourselves. You have to realize that things don't always go according to plan. And besides all you would've got working for Motown would have been a paycheck."

"What do you mean? You guys are the ones who suggested me interning over there," stormed rich rapper with a confused look on his face.

"The only reason why we recommended joining Motown was to learn the business from people with years of experience. We weren't expecting you to be looking to climb the corporate ladder."

"I don't understand" replied rich rapper, scratching his head as he tried to hide the dumb founded look in his face.

The entrepreneurs boomed, "Listen closely to what we're telling you. This could make all the difference in your life. If you want to make yacht money, you've got to start looking at the world through a different pair of eyes. Climbing the corporate ladder at any company is just like looking for a record deal. It gives the company you work for more control over your life. If you don't believe us, ask somebody with a high paying job not to go to work for a month without calling in sick. Chances are that person might not have a job to go back to."

"Ok, so what you're telling me is that job security and record deals are good for most people but the price they have to pay is being told what to do by someone else" replied rich rapper.

"Good, you're starting to see the other side of the coin" replied the entrepreneurs. "Taking control over your life and not having anyone telling you what to do is the key to finding yacht money. The point we want you to understand is that when you're working hard at a job for a pay check, that's all life gives you. A pay check which is usually depleted the moment you get it because you have bills to pay. Don't you know that those same bills you find yourself paying are making somebody else richer?"

Rich rapper could see where this conversation was headed. The entrepreneurs where trying to tell him that if he takes control over his own life, he wouldn't have to depend on a pay check from the label. He would have control over his own lively hood plus be in a position to do as he pleases with both his time and music.

The entrepreneurs continued "Why don't you be the person that owns the company which sends out bills to be paid? In your case you want to be a successful rapper. Why not build a record label? Enter the music business through the back door man."

The thought of building a record company intimidated rich rapper. How on earth was he going to build a record label? It seemed like an impossible task.

"Building a company is difficult and doesn't that take a lot of money?" he asked. Rich rapper had always thought of himself as a person who wasn't business minded. He had never done anything along those lines. So he continued his whining, "Building a label takes a lot of work and I don't have a business degree. I also don't have connections in the music industry."

The entrepreneurs observed rich rapper in his self imposed state of helplessness and boomed "Yes, building a business takes a lot of hard work but if I'm not mistaken, you are the one that asked us to teach you how make yacht money. Saying you don't have connections and collage degrees are excuses you're making to stop yourself from doing what you know you have to do. Many of the most successful entrepreneurs never had business degrees and connections when they started. They used the little they had and made the best out of every situation."

Deep down inside rich rapper knew the entrepreneurs were right. He was trying to avoid doing what he knew he had to do. Life had handed him an unfair hand but it was up to him to change the hand he was dealt.

As if on scrip he reflected on his life and realized that he didn't stand a chance of getting a high paying job at any major label. He didn't have the qualifications companies pay big bucks for. Even if he was lucky enough to get into Motown, the business affairs manager would most lightly do everything within her power to block him from being promoted since she wanted one of her friends to get the internship.

Rich rapper also realized that he had been making good music for more than eleven years but had nothing to show for it. He and poor rapper were still on their hands and knees begging for a major record deal. It's no secret that out of the millions of talented artists in the world, only a few ever get a major deal. The sad thing about the ones that are lucky enough to get signed is that most of them don't make any money off their own record sales. They usually find themselves mad at the record company for making hundreds of millions of dollars while they are still recouping. Life sure can be a bitch!

The entrepreneurs were right. The best chance rich rapper had of becoming successful was to build his record company. He didn't necessarily have to have a collage degree hanging on his wall to start building his business. Having the guts to get started was all he needed to be on his way. He liked the thought of being free to make his version of real hip hop without anybody telling him what to do.

He then reassured the entrepreneurs that he was willing to learn whatever he had to learn to become a positive, rich entrepreneur who could do as he pleases with his music.

The entrepreneurs smiled as they saw the spark in rich rappers eyes and said "Welcome to the road less traveled. Many people have failed along the way but we believe you can make it. You don't have the experience yet, but if you're willing to learn and make mistakes along the way, you'll do just fine. Success only comes to those who are willing sacrifice their time, money, and efforts. If you're willing to pay the price of success, a new world of abundance will open up to you."

Rich rapper knew the entrepreneurs were not in his line of business but they helped him make the decision to become a successful rapper who didn't need a record deal to succeed.

Author's Notes

I strongly recommend checking out our online support system at _www.richrapper.com_. Our website is designed to help independent rappers sell their CD's, downloads and merchandise (T-shirts, DVD's, hats etc) directly to their customers.

Not only do we help you create an income with your music, but you can also get paid through other artist's music. How's that for big pimping huh? We believe in you because we know you have what it takes to be successful with your music.

BEGINNINGS

CHAPTER 7

Overcoming Criticism

By the time rich rapper got back to Florida his frame of mind had begun to change. He was no longer seeking a record deal and wanted to build his own record company. He also knew the risks involved in building his own business and no matter what happened in his personal life, he was determined to make his business work.

Unfortunately rich rappers friends didn't feel the same way. Poor rapper was disappointed because rich rapper didn't come back with a major record deal. He had invested so much time making beats for rich rapper and the idea of building a business didn't appeal to him. Poor rapper was only interested in being famous and getting paid. Building a label was out of the question.

When rich rapper tried to explain what he had learnt from the entrepreneurs, poor rapper laughed at him. He said things like "Why don't you get a record deal like everyone else? Do you think you are better than everyone else? What makes you think you can build a label when you don't even have a car to get from point A to point B?"

The laughter and ridicule from friends had rich rapper feeling discouraged, but what hurt the most was the criticism from his, own family. When he spoke of building a business, they would silently laugh at him behind his back. In their opinion, he was just another kid with wild dreams which will never come true. It's sad but that's the harsh reality most entrepreneurs face before their dreams take flight.

Nobody ever said the road to success would be easy but if you're willing to overcome challenges, you'll have your hearts deepest desires. I wish I could tell you that finding success has been easy for rich rapper. The honest truth is that it hasn't been easy and rich rapper still hasn't accomplished everything he set out to do. He is however, well on his way to becoming the entrepreneur he dreams about being.

If the advice rich rapper received from the entrepreneurs is appealing to you, you're going to have to prepare for the criticism ahead. Not everybody is going to understand what you've set out to do. Some of your own family members and friends are going to laugh at you because they might not see the future you see for yourself. Don't let them discourage you. Stick to your guns and keep pushing forward until you become the successful artist you want to become. There will be times when you feel like giving up but don't do it. Winners hang in there no matter what people many say or think about them.

One thing you always have to remember is that whenever you set your own mark in life, you will attract critics. The critics always have something to say about you, no matter what you do. It's almost like they get a sense of accomplishment from trying to stop you from doing what you know you have to do.

Take a close look at your life to see if you're attracting critics. If you're not attracting them, I strongly suggest working harder on your music and finding innovative ways of selling it. Think of the critics as people that acknowledge your existence. It's better to have them talking about you and your music than them not mentioning your name.

Rich rapper had to learn this lesson the hard way when he released his debut album. He thought everyone was going to love his music but that was not the case. Instead of getting critical acclaim he was ridiculed. They didn't waist any time tearing him down.

The negative comments hurt his feelings but the more the critics talked about rich rappers music, the more units he ended up selling. Thanks to the critics hard efforts. I'm sure rich rapper appreciates the business.

Don't be afraid of them. Regardless of whether their comments sound good or bad, just make sure you have people talking about your music.

CHAPTER 8

Overcoming

Doubt

We all have a little coward inside us that is afraid to start something new. Every time we find the courage to step into the world of the unknown, the little coward taps us on the shoulder and snickers "You're not smart enough to accomplish what you've set out to do"

Sometimes the little coward whispers statements like "That will never work! If it is such a good idea, how come no one else is doing it? You're not a savvy entrepreneur. You don't even have a business degree."

Rich rapper had to confront the little coward inside him before he could move forward. The odds were against him because he never had a collage degree, he had never built a successful business and he never had the start up capital to launch his record company. The little coward inside him, along with the criticism from some of his family and friends left him feeling discouraged.

After many sleepless nights and wondering whether to continue pursuing his dreams, rich rapper was forced to make a decision that would affect his life forever.

He had to either control his own destiny in the music business independently or beg for a major record deal like everybody else. This is a decision that has to be made by every artist that takes their music seriously. Do you want to call your own shots or do you want someone with a corporate job to tell you what kind of music to make?

Rich rapper chose to call his, own shots. He knew that windows of opportunity would open up for him if he started selling a lot of records independently. Major labels are looking to work with established or independent artists because they don't have to developing them. Artist development costs them a lot of money and we all know that the majors are only interested in making money.

Having control of his own career encouraged rich rapper to start building an independent record company. Even if he chose to work with major record labels in the future, things would be on his own terms since nobody would be in a position to tell him what to do.

Rich rapper is no better than you. He's a regular guy, just like you, who chose to change the hand he was dealt. If rich rapper could overcome his doubts you can do it too. All you have to do is just step out of your comfort zone and step into the grey area.

Nothing in life is guaranteed but I can promise you that if you want to excel beyond average, you will have to be willing to do the things most artists don't want to do.

An effective way to overcome doubt and fear is to carefully watch what you put into your mind. How can you do that you ask me?

Well, you can start by reading books that inspire you to keep pushing forward in spite of whatever challenges you will have to overcome. I know the thought of reading might not appeal to some of us, but the truth is, you are what you read.

If you go to collage and all you read are books about the law, chances are you'll wind up being a lawyer. If all you read are books about cutting hair, chances are you'll become a hair dresser.

The same applies to the music business. Be careful about the material you put into your mind because it will determine your future.

I've often heard a wise people say "You can tell a persons past, present and future by listening to their choice of words." Words are so powerful because they reflect our thoughts. It's no secret that everything we do started out as a thought which we chose to act upon. It might be a good idea to watch your thoughts closely. They can either be helping you accomplish your goals or pushing you further away from your dreams.

Getting Started

CHAPTER 9

Getting Started

Rich rapper started taking control of his career when many people thought it couldn't be done. He had the courage to find within himself, what many people consider an impossible dream and start turning that dream into reality. If he could find the courage to get started, you can do it too.

You have a genius inside of you that is waiting to be called upon. The potential to take your music to the next level is within you, but the decision to get started is yours. I offer you the following 6 steps as a process to help you develop your God given abilities.

1) Needing a Reason Lager than Reality:

Everything we do in life is attached to a strong reason. If we set out to do anything without a purpose, we are bound to fail.

Life's challenges have a way of presenting themselves when we set out to do great things. When these obstacles present themselves, many people don't have the courage to keep moving forward. The people who decide to keep plunging forward, even when the night looks hopeless are the ones with a reason that is larger than reality. They see possibilities for themselves, which nobody else can see for them.

No matter what may happen around them, they are willing to do whatever it takes to turn the vision they have in their minds into reality. The reason behind why they dedicate themselves to accomplishing their goals is what gets them through the rough times. That's what makes the difference between people with a reason larger than reality and people who don't.

2) Choosing Daily: We are what we are today, because of the decisions we have made along life's journey. Every decision we've made has affected our lives in either a negative or positive way. The differences between rich rapper and poor rapper are mainly found in their train of thought. They are both very talented artists but their core beliefs are completely different.
They both want to do well for themselves but the choices they make daily make all the difference. Their thoughts reflect whether they want to own the company that releases their music or if they want to be at the mercy of the record company that releases their music.

These are the decisions that every artist makes on a daily basis. It's up to you choose which train of thought is going to determine your future.

3) Choose Friends Carefully: I don't remember exactly where I read a book that stated "You'll be the same person in five years with the exception of two things: The people you associate with and the books that you read." That profound statement has stuck with me ever since.

The power of association is incredible. The people you spend most of your time with are either helping you advance to your next higher level, or they're stopping you from growing.

When rich rapper decided to take control of his career and start his business, he was faced with violent opposition from poor rapper and some of his old friends. For some strange reason poor rapper and company, couldn't imagine rich rapper building a successful business.

The thought of rich rapper achieving such a goal was unrealistic to them. So they did the only thing that seemed logical to them. They laughed at rich rapper and kept trying to discourage him. Rich rapper tried convincing his friends to join him, but his friends chose to walk a different path. They obviously didn't want to change.

The road less traveled is hard and not everyone is willing to move in that direction. I wish I could tell you that poor rapper changed his mind and decided to team up with rich rapper to build a business. Unfortunately, things didn't work out that way. Rich rapper and poor rapper began distancing themselves from each other. Their core beliefs began to change and a world of different realities began to open up for both of them.

You might be ready to make some positive new changes in your life but if your friends are holding you back, you might have to do what rich rapper did. He put it upon himself to find new friends that supported the changes he was making.

4) Pay Your Advisors Well: I have come across many independent rappers that can't stand the thought of paying their advisors well. Poor rapper doesn't like paying his advisors either. He tries to stiff his manager and lawyer every time he can, so he may have extra spending money for himself.

Rich rapper does the complete opposite. While poor rapper is looking for ways to save money through stiffing his advisors, rich rapper is looking for ways to make more money through his advisors advice.

Rich rapper believes his advisors are more knowledgeable than he is in certain areas so he pays them well. The long term benefits of paying them well will take you a lot further than you trying to do everything on your own. Life is a lot easier for people who work together as a team. Be a team player who's leading his team of advisors to victory.

5) Find Hero's To Admire: Every great leader was once a great student that learnt everything he could from his mentors. Wise students study their mentors every move. A mentor can be anybody that is more successful than you are in a specific area. However, the type of mentors I'm referring to are the hero's that society consider lager than life. People like Donald Trump, P Diddy, Damon Dash, Russell Simmons and Jay Z are perfect examples. They make living the good life look easy. The money, fame, cars, and women, they have are enough to make any man satisfied with all the earthly pleasures life has to offer.

Now I can already hear some people screaming "I'm not really interested in money. Why is this world so materialistic?"

I'm not all about money either. The reason why I recommend finding hero's to admire is simply to have you thinking bigger than where you are right now.

Your hero's could be can be spiritual leaders, political leaders or people from whatever walk of life you can relate to. Only you have the power to decide the life path that is right for you. But let me remind you that the people you look up to are consciously or unconsciously helping you mold your lifestyle. Pick your hero's wisely because your future is slowly being determined by the advice you choose to take from your hero's.

Use the Power of Giving: Poor rapper is an artist that says he wants to help the poor when he gets extra cash. He has good intentions but the harsh reality is that he almost never has extra money to give away. He usually finds himself broke at the end of every month after paying his bills.

Rich rapper sometimes has cash flow problems but he makes it a point to give ten percent of the money he makes to his church or a charitable organization he believes in. In his opinion giving away that ten percent does not take money out of his pocket. Instead, he sees it as an investment that helps him get extra cash.

Don't be afraid to give because the more you give, the more you'll receive. That goes for anything in life. If you want a smile, smile at someone else first and you will receive one back. If you want money do the same thing and you will be sure to receive it back with interest.

Start Right Now!

CHAPTER 10

Start Right Now!

I've decided to add a few to do's to help you get stated on your journey as an independent artist. I wish I could tell you the road ahead was easy for rich rapper, but it wasn't. He had to go through a lot of heart ache and pain to grow into the person he is today. Like I said before, if rich rapper had the courage to get started, you can do it to. Here are some to do's.

- Stop what you are doing right now! And make an honest assessment about your progress. Find out what is working for you. It makes no sense to keep hanging on to old ideas that no longer work. If what you're doing right now is not giving you the results you want, then maybe it's time to make some changes. Look at the results you are getting to discover what's working.

- Start reading books and magazines that offer something of value to your life. The more books you read, the more you grow. To become a leader in your industry, you have to be aware of the changes that can affect your business. You've got to be prepared to take the necessary action that needs to be taken so you can advance to the next level.

Rich rapper is a man that kept reading, even after he dropped out of collage as a straight "C" student. Long after many of his peers had graduated from school and put aside their books, rich rapper kept reading.

He considered his mind to be the most valuable asset in his possession. He believes in studying to better himself, not to impress some collage professors or employers who only offer job security.

• Find people who have done what you want to do and learn everything you can from them. These are the mentors that can point you in the right direction since they have been where you want to go. It's a lot easier to learn from their mistakes. You'll accomplish your goals a lot quicker if you only listen to what they have to say.

If you don't have direct access to your hero's, you can always read biographies, autobiographies and articles about them. Learn everything you can about these wonderful people.

• Take classes and buy tapes about business and investing. I can't express how important these subjects are to your financial future if you plan on building your own business.

Building a successful business that can help you take your music to the next level is going to require all your time and energy. Make sure you take the time to learn all you can from tapes, classes and seminars, and then apply it to your business. It makes no sense to learn about business if you're not going to apply it in the real world.

• Train your mind to see opportunities many people can't see. The best deals are made by people who see what most people don't see. Think independently and don't always think of doing things in the traditional way. It isn't, always the best way to get things done.

The music industry is structured in a way that almost everyone follows. Know the traditional rules and find ways to legally stretch them.

I'm not suggesting breaking the law, so please don't do something that will get you locked up. I'm simply suggesting using your imagination to put the odds in your favor. The world is your stage. Don't be afraid to think outside the box. You don't have to do what everyone else is doing.

• Don't worry about getting a record deal anymore. Put it upon yourself to create your own lucky breaks and do whatever you must to get your music out to the masses. Make copies of your CD and start sell them to everyone that is interested in what you have to offer. Don't be afraid of selling. Phone companies, super markets, and adult movie stores all sell their products to the public. You can do the same with your music.

Putting your music on movie soundtracks and video games, plus doing live shows will help you sell more CDs. I also recommend taking advantage of is the internet. It has the potential of reaching many customers around the world, who might have never known about your wonderful music.

I strongly recommend visiting our website www.richrapper.com. This website was designed to help you sell your music on the internet, without signing your life away. Unlike major record labels, we allow you to keep 100 percent ownership of your music and we're non exclusive.

Now that I've given you some to do's, it's up to you to go out there and take the world by storm. This book is just a guide to help you get started. Once you start taking action, you will discover many more new ways of exposing your music.

Keep experimenting until you find what works best for you. Your career is in your hands but the question is, what are you going to do with it?

Start taking action right now!

Epilogue

Both rich rapper and poor rapper are not signed to major record companies today. Rich rapper is still building his business. He has released one independent album which is doing reasonably well, and is working on the second one. The world isn't singing his songs yet, but I guess it's safe to say he's on his way.

Poor rapper on the other hand, still hasn't released a CD yet. He's currently trying to get signed to an independent label that supposedly has ties with popular artists on TVT records. Only time will tell what will come out of his efforts. I hope he gets the record deal he's after.

Both rich rapper and poor rapper still have big dreams. The challenges of life haven't stopped either one of them from working their way into the music business. Sadly, it hurts me to report the major differences that have occurred between both rappers.

Rich rapper is no longer looking for a record deal because his record company releases his music. Poor rapper finds himself submitting his demo package to record companies, hoping they give him a record deal.

Rich rapper is receiving payments from customers who are buying his music since it's available in select retail outlets. Poor rapper isn't making any money with his music because he is waiting for a label to sign him.

Poor rapper also has a nasty attitude towards money. He's always quoting a biblical verse that states "The love of money is the root of all evil." In his opinion, money is evil and it makes people do evil things. I have often heard him mumble "Money can't buy you love" and "I'd rather be poor and happy than rich and unhappy."

It's funny how life tends to give us what we ask for. If you look at poor rappers accomplishments today, you will discover that he really is poor and happy, making music which isn't generating an income for him.

When it comes to the subject of money, rich rappers point of view is almost the complete opposite. If you ask him what he thinks about the biblical verse "The love of money is the root of all evil." His reply would be "Yes, the love of money is the root of all evil. Poverty makes people rob, steal, and kill, just to get their hands on a little money. If a person wasn't in poverty, why would they want to harm other people for a few bucks?"

He would go on to say "I don't believe money on its own is either good or bad. It's the individual that's good or bad. That's why the key words in that biblical verse are **'the love of money**.' I've yet to hear a hundred dollar bill speak to me. Only a person can decide to do good or evil deeds with their money. Money doesn't have a mind of its own."

Rich rapper often hears poor rapper screaming "I would rather be poor and happy, than rich and unhappy." So he no longer tries to change poor rappers thinking, since it only leads to an argument. Instead he whispers to himself "If poor rapper only knew that he could be both rich and happy. Life would be more comfortable for him and his loved ones. Being a rich and happy person sounds a lot better than being a poor and happy individual."

I often speak to highly successful people who all agree that emotions like joy and sadness have nothing to do with an individual's finances. Most of them even go on to explain that they've been, rich and poor, happy and unhappy. And life was even more miserable for them when they were poor and unhappy. Being rich and happy is more appealing to them because they have more control over their lives and when emergencies arrive, they have the money to take care of whatever problems they might be facing. Money is just a tool that they use to make their lives more comfortable.

As an artist, you have to decide which path is right for you. Rich rappers path is difficult at first, but it gets easier when you start learning the basics. Poor rappers path works well for many rappers at first. But if things don't go according to plan, life can get very complicated in the long run.

There's no right or wrong way of getting your music out there. The main thing that will make the difference is what you will accomplish at the end of the road. Will you be at the mercy of a record label, or will you be in control of your own music?

About The Author

Hilary Mujikwa is a rugged entrepreneur that has been working with independent hip hop artists since 1993.

His main focus is helping independent rappers sell their music because he was once an independent rapper himself. He knows how difficult it is for up and coming artists to establish themselves as household names in hip hop. So for that very same reason, he put it upon himself to help aspiring rappers sell their music through www.richrapper.com, a digital music outlet created for the sole purpose of helping independent rappers sell their downloads, CD's and merchandise on the World Wide Web. Please feel free to visit our website for more information.